The

DEAD POETS'
CABARET

David Cobb

*A celebration of dead Anglophone poets from
the British Isles, with the circumstances of their
deaths and burials, pictures of their graves,
and clerihews and other light verses
by the book's author.*

**IRON
PRESS**

First published April 2003 by IRON Press
5 Marden Tce, Cullercoats, Northumberland
England, NE30 4PD
Tel/Fax: +44 (0) 191 253 1901
Email: seaboy@freenetname.co.uk
website: www.ironpress.co.uk

ISBN 0 906228 88 3

FIRST EDITION

cover and book design by IRONeye @ IRON Press
cover photo Zoe Savina

copy editor Michael Wilkin

IRON Press books are distributed by Central Books

IRON Press is represented by
Inpress Ltd
1st Floor
52 Harpur St
Bedford
MK40 2QT
Tel: +44 (0)1234 330023
Fax: +44 (0) 1234 330024
Email: jon@inpressbooks.co.uk
Web: www.inpressbooks.co.uk

SUPPORTED BY
THE NATIONAL LOTTERY
THROUGH
THE ARTS COUNCIL
OF ENGLAND

northern
arts
PROMOTING THE ARTS
IN THE NORTH

for COLIN BLUNDELL

Acknowledgements

In addition to the Dictionary of National Biography (DNB), I am indebted to several works for a quantity of interesting information, and therefore grateful to the researchers who compiled them. They are:

D Greenwood, *Who's Buried Where in England?* (third edition), pub. Constable, 1999.
M Kerrigan, *Who Lies Where?*, pub. Fourth Estate, 1998.
M Schmidt, *Lives of the Poets*, pub. Weidenfeld & Nicolson, 1998.
J Sutherland, *The Oxford Book of Literary Anecdotes*, pub. OUP, 1987.
Samuel Johnson, *Lives of the English Poets*, ed. Arthur Waugh, pub. Kegan, Paul, 1896, and a Selection of the same, pub. Everyman, 1975.
A Motion, 1993, *Philip Larkin, A Writer's Life.*
E Feinstein, 2001, *Ted Hughes, the Life of a Poet.*

The following provided various kinds of help and I am grateful to them for it: the Berkshire Record Office, the Commonwealth War Graves Commission, the Library of Westminster Abbey, Nailsworth Town Archives, Carole Brough of Mole Valley District Council, the Brecknock Museum, the Dumfries Museum, Heather Kirk, Georges Friedenkraft, William J Higginson, Treasa Macmanus, Zoe Savina, Graham High, Philip Hoskins, Madeleine Holroyd, Mrs Jean B Pateman and Malin Forsell of the Friends of Highgate Cemetery, Isolde Schäfer, Mara Zavagno, and the anonymous vicars, organists, vergers, caretakers, helpers, gardeners, people in the street, and the man in the Gray's Inn Road with a ring through his nose, all of whom at one time or another dealt kindly with dumb questions.

Who can sufficiently thank a great poet,
the most precious jewel of a nation?

Ludwig van Beethoven

By the same author:

(from IRON Press)

Jumping from Kiyomizu
The Iron Book of British Haiku (ed. with Martin Lucas)

(from Equinox Press)

Palm
The Spring Journey to the Saxon Shore

(from The British Museum Press)

The British Museum Haiku

CONTENTS

FOREWORD

This is a compendium of information about the circumstances of death of eighty Anglophone poets of the British Isles, how they were buried or otherwise disposed of, and in many cases what happened to them later.

Like the run of us, many of these poets died hard deaths: in poverty (one poet choked on a piece of bread he had begged), of unpleasant illnesses, blown up on battlefields, drowned, perhaps even by their own hands, denied in life the recognition they won after their deaths. Nor were they always buried as they wished.

Only about one in seven of these poets ever made it 'in person' to Poets' Corner in Westminster Abbey, or to St Paul's Cathedral, though they may subsequently have had a memorial put up for them in one of those grand shrines. The large majority lie at rest in relatively obscure places, such as country churchyards, or public cemeteries under the aegis of (believe it or not!) communal 'Leisure Service Departments'. They may or may not often be visited, and their graves are in various states of repair.

'Last resting place?' A hollow phrase. Leaving aside those who were divided into pieces and put in more than one grave (Hardy, Shelley), and the ones who were disturbed by souvenir hunters (Milton, Byron), no less than eight of the poets in this volume were buried in one place, only to be disinterred and reburied somewhere else: Burns, Chatterton, Coleridge, Donne and Sir Philip Sidney (the last two after being burnt out), Earl of Surrey, Wilde and Yeats (to which one might add Goldsmith, who was presumably shaken severely in his safe haven by a bomb in the London blitz.)

Some of us find it inspirational to reflect on these ups and downs of a poet's existence, both as a living and a dead being. We like to stand for a few moments at a graveside and thank the poet for the uplift his or her poetry has given us. This book may prompt a few more of us to look them up.

Let the Scots 'tak' the high road' and knock off the Munroes, their bens over three-thousand feet in altitude, we English will 'tak' the low road' (actually a euphemism for being put six feet under) and count up the poets we have put to bed! I shall not boast about my own tally, a mere sixtyfive of them so far, for with the aid of this vade mecum I'm sure you have it in you to beat this score.

Often as not, the inscription on a poet's tomb ends with the word Poet instead of the familiar RIP. 'There's no peace for the wicked,' my mother used to say. I won't press the syllogism.

Such encounters between the living and the 'living dead' shouldn't be mournful ones. To this end I hope the addition of a clerihew or other light verse in each case, maybe extravagantly apocryphal and maybe not, but as Gavin Ewart pointed out, always 'free from malice', will draw us further into a jovial community with them. The poet's cry of 'Rejoice!' is more convincing than any politician's ever was.

As to the clerihew, not a widely practised poetic form, a word may need to be said. G K Chesterton considered it a 'severe and stately form of free verse'. Gavin Ewart thought it 'civilised and dotty.' E C Bentley himself, the form's inventor, observed with an air of surprise, 'in course of time it seemed to find its way into the hands of connoisseurs of idiocy everywhere.'

Some of the 'light verses' in this book are not strictly true to the perceived rules of clerihew. They err towards the double-couplet jingle. I admit this to save anyone the trouble of pointing it out. The simple fact is, either I was working under more constraints than usual, with a predetermined cast of characters; or I am just not very good at clerihews. But I can illustrate the sort of choice I had to make. Take Moore as an example.

The following strict clerihew was possible:

7

MATTHEW ARNOLD

Died of heart failure, Liverpool, 1888, age 65. Buried All Saints churchyard, Laleham, Surrey. Memorial in Westminster Abbey.

Inscriptions: (at Laleham) *'Matthew Arnold, eldest son of the late Thomas Arnold D.D. Head Master of Rugby School. There is sprung up a light for the righteous and joyful gladness for such as are true-hearted.' (in Westminster Abbey): 'Let but the light appear And thy transfigured walls be touch'd with flame.'*

**Matthew Arnold
Had no one to darn old
Socks, until he kissed
A masochist.**

W(ystan) H(ugh) AUDEN

Died 1973, age 65, of a heart attack, following a reading of his poems to the Austrian Society of Literature, on the way to his alternative home in Oxford. Had a morbid fear of isolation and dying where he might not be discovered for a week. A Viennese hotel with room service saved him from that. Buried in the churchyard at his summer home, Kirchstetten, 28 miles west of Vienna. Wagner's Siegfried Idyll was played at his funeral; the street leading to his villa in Kirchstetten had been named in his lifetime, *W.-H.-Audenstrasse.*

Inscriptions: (on memorial in Christ Church Cathedral, Oxford) 'Bless what there is for being.' (on memorial in Westminster Abbey):
'In the prison of his days
Teach the free man how to praise.'

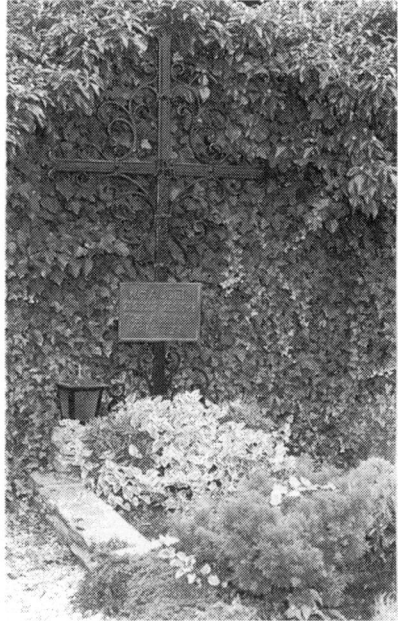

You could tell Auden
Was rather modern
Simply by the look of the man:
Lines on his physog didn't scan.

WILLIAM BARNES

Died 1886, age 85. Buried by the disused church of St Peter's, Winterborne Came, Dorset, under an eight-foot Celtic cross. Mourned locally for making patriotic use of the Dorset dialect in his poems, he also campaigned against words with Latin or Greek roots, e.g. preferring sunprint (Dor. zunprint) to photograph (Dor. votograph). Statue erected to him outside St Peter's, Dorchester.

Inscriptions: (on cross) ND. (under statue) 'Zoo now I hope this kindly feace Is gone to vind a better pleace But still wi' vo'k a-left behind He'll always be a-kept in mind.'

**The empire of William Barnes
Was smaller than Genghis Khan's,
Restricting him, like a corset,
To Dorset.**

HILAIRE BELLOC

Died 1953, age 82, in Guildford Hospital. Buried in the church-yard of Our Lady of Consolation and St Francis, West Grinstead, Sussex. Burial plot hedged with box, timber headboard with ceramic inset of Virgin and Child. Following a stroke, the poet, famous for his Cautionary Tales with gory endings, fell into an open fire while attempting to poke it. His own famous epitaph doesn't appear on the grave: 'When I am dead, I hope it may be said, His sins were scarlet, but his books were read.'

Inscriptions: (on a tablet by a door) 'Five yards east of this stone lies the body of Hilaire Belloc, for 48 years a member of the congregation of this Church of Our Lady of Consolation, in whose memory this tower and spire were completed in 1964 in grateful recognition of his zealous and unwavering profession of our Holy Faith which he defended in his writings and noble verse. This is the Faith that I have held and hold and This is That in which I mean to die.' (on the headboard) ND

**No one annoyed Hilaire Belloc
More than those who can't tell hoc
From hic.
Any abuse of Latin made him sic.**

EDWARD BENLOWES

Died 1676, age 73, in an apothecary's house, during an epidemic 'of malignant feaver'. Buried St Mary the Virgin's Church, Oxford, according to a contemporary account, 'under the north wall ... his head neare to the entrance of the vestry ... accompanied with the bishop and certain Drs to his grave.' Alas, his head is now under a paved step leading to a coffee room, with a trap for cockroaches planted on top and a row of dustbins at his feet. Reckless generosity to fellow poets, vanities of self-publishing, and fines for supporting the Royalist cause, reduced him from great wealth to abject poverty, so that he died 'for want of conveniences fit for old age, as clothes, fewell, and warm things to refresh the body.' He wrote habitually in a stanza form unique to himself.

Inscription: None.

If he'd known Bashô, Benlowes
Might have thought the haiku quelque-chose.
But for him the thirty-syllable triolet
Was inviolate.

SIR JOHN BETJEMAN

Died of Parkinson's disease, 1984, age 78. Buried in St
Enodoc's churchyard, Trebetherick, North Cornwall.
(Approached across tenth hole fairway of local golf course, grave
is near south side of church.)

*Inscription: In absence of any on the tombstone we quote this
verse by the poet himself: 'Blessed be St Enodoc, Blessed be the
wave, Blessed be the springy turf, We pray, we pray to thee!'*

A cautious employer, Betjeman
Warned about butlers, 'Better vet your man!'
A maxim his saluki
Found spooky.

WILLIAM BLAKE

Died 1827, age 69. Buried Bunhill Fields, Finsbury, London (exact whereabouts unknown). Memorial in crypt of St Paul's and bust in Westminster Abbey. Suffered in final year from 'ague'. Spent last hours drawing his wife, retouching a print of The Ancient of Days, and singing 'Hallelujahs and songs of joy and triumph ... with ecstatic energy, ... happy that he had run his race.' A friend commented, "I have been at the death, not of a man, but of a blessed angel."

Inscription: (in St Paul's) 'Artist Poet Mystic. To see a world in a grain of sand And a heaven in a wild flower Hold infinity in the palm of your hand And eternity in an hour.'

**The views of Blake
On nakedness were not opaque.
Thought it very far from rude
To write his poems in the nude.**

ROBERT BLOOMFIELD

Died 1823, age 56, half-blind, in great poverty. DNB assertion that, had he not died then, he would soon have gone mad, is disputed. Buried All Saints' churchyard, Campton, Nr. Shefford, Bedfordshire. Debut volume of poetry, The Farmer's Boy, based on his own experiences, reputed to have sold 26,000 copies in less than three years. Being too frail for farmwork he became a shoemaker and later manufactured Aeolian harps.

Inscription: '*Here lie the remains of (ND) ... Let his wild native wood notes tell the rest.*'

Country life for Bloomfield
Was far from gloom-filled,
But it's quite incredible
He thought turnips so edible!

EDMUND BLUNDEN

Died 1974, age 77. In poor health for years before his death. Buried in Holy Trinity churchyard, Long Melford, Suffolk. At his funeral his old battalion runner laid a wreath of Flanders poppies on the coffin.

Inscription: (from his own poem) 'I live still, to love still Things quiet and unconcerned.'

**Edmund Blunden
Skedaddled from London
To teach haijin in Hiroshima
Terza rima.**

ROBERT BRIDGES

Died 1930, age 85. A Latin monument inside St Peter and St Paul's Church, Yattendon, Berkshire, relates that his ashes were deposited close to a cross he had erected in the nearby churchyard, over the body of his mother (Harriet Elizabeth Affleck) of whom he was one of 55 descendants of her first marriage when she died. Such a cross is no longer visible. Poet Laureate, 1913-30; co-founder, Society for Pure English; composer of *The Yattendon Hymnal*; a medical man.

A meticulous clinician, Bridges
Sewed people up with scanning stitches.
Anapaests for private patients;
Iambs for their poor relations.

EMILY BRONTË

Died of consumption, 1848, age 30. Uncomplaining by nature, she wouldn't see a doctor until she was near to death; on the day itself she got up as usual, dressed, and went about her duties. Buried St Michael and All Angels' Church, Haworth, Yorkshire (beneath the one-time family pew, in a vault she shares with seven others of the Brontë family.) Charlotte Brontë described her sister as 'turning her dying eyes reluctantly from the pleasant sun', and Emily's 'house-dog' followed the cortege.

Inscriptions: (in the vault, and not peculiar to her) 'The sting of death is sin, and the strength of sin is the law; but thanks be to God which giveth us the victory through our Lord Jesus Christ.' (memorial in Westminster Abbey) 'With courage to endure.'

**Emily Brontë
Despised 'the full Monty'.
She preferred sights
Such as Wuthering Heights.**

RUPERT BROOKE

Died 1915, age 27, on troopship bound for Gallipoli, of blood poisoning aggravated by sunstroke. Buried by comrades on Greek island of Skyros in an isolated grave in an olive grove on east side of Tris Boukes Bay, under a makeshift cairn of stones, replaced later by his mother with a marble monument. On nearby headland there is also a fine memorial by Michalis Tombros (1930) overlooking the sea. Model for this statue was a young Greek dancer, Alexander Iolas (misrepresented in anecdote as 'a male prostitute from Antwerp.') Brooke left royalties to establish his literary friends, Abercrombie, Gibson and De la Mare.

Inscription: *(tr. from Greek) 'And now having seen the holy land of Attika I can die.'*

**At teatime, Brooke
Sought for himself some quiet nook.
In many a corner, lying waste
Are sandwiches of sardine paste.**

ELIZABETH BARRETT BROWNING

Died of a severe chill, 1861, age 55. Mourning for Cavour is said
to have hastened her death. Buried Cimitero degli Inglesi,
Florence, Italy. She had lived there with her husband, Robert
Browning, since their elopement and marriage.

*Inscription: The municipality of Florence placed a tablet in her
memory in the walls of Casa Guidi. It reads: Qui scrisse e mori
E.B.B., che in un cuore di donna conciliava scienze di dotto e
spirito di poeta e fece del suo verso aureo, anello tra Italia e
Inghilterra. Pose questa memoria, grata, Firenze, 1861.*

**A phrase disliked by Ms Barrett
Was 'sick as a parrot'.
She assured people life on a sofa
Made her sick as a gopher.**

ROBERT BROWNING

Died after catching cold in Venice, 1889, age 77. The cemetery in Florence where his wife was buried was closed to further burials, so he was interred at Westminster Abbey, London (in the south transept.) His final book of poetry was published the day he died.

Inscription: ND

**No use was Browning
To a girl who was drowning.
Her frantic hand he couldn't clasp;
He said his reach outstretched his grasp.**

ROBERT BURNS

Died of fever, 1796, age 37. Buried first in St Michael's church-yard, Dumfries, Scotland, in a corner tomb which the tourist guide calls 'modest', then in 1815 transferred to a Grecian Mausoleum which it calls 'more fitting'. During last illness, 'His humour was unruffled, and his wit never forsook him. He looked to one of his fellow volunteers with a smile ... and said, "Don't let the awkward squad fire over me." He repressed with a smile the hopes of his friends, and told them he had lived long enough.' (Lockhart, 1828.) Memorial in Westminster Abbey.

Inscription: 'The remains of Burns removed into the vault below, 19th Sept 1815.' Also recorded are his wife, Jean Armour, and three of his sons, who are buried with him.

Robert Burns
Made ingenious tax returns.
His claims for children's benefits
Had the inspectors doing splits.

GEORGE GORDON, LORD BYRON

Died of swamp fever, Missolonghi, Greece,1824, age 36. Interred
St Mary Magdalen Church, Hucknall, Nottinghamshire, in the
family vault. Over-zealous bleeding by doctors may have con-
tributed to his death. Byron did not want to be buried in England:
'I believe the thought could drive me mad on my deathbed.' John
Clare saw his funeral '... by chance as I was wandering up
Oxford Street ... a young girl that stood by me gave a deep sigh
and uttered, "Poor Lord Byron," and I looked up at the young
girl's face. It was dark and beautiful, and I could almost feel in
love with her for the sigh she had uttered for the poet ... she told
me there were sixty-three or four (carriages) in all ...the gilt ones
that led the procession were empty ... the hearse looked rather
small and rather mean and the coach that carried his embers in an
urn (sic) over which a pall was thrown.' The church displays a
wreath from Byron's coffin and other mementoes, together with
quotations from his poem, Childe Harold's Pilgrimage. In Athens,
there is a marble statue of Byron close to the Acropolis.
In 1938, the Byron vault was opened by the vicar in secrecy. In a
very tight chamber (7'6" x 6'0") he found twenty-seven members
of the Byron family packed, and identified what he believed must
be the poet's oak coffin, still in very good condition, except that
the identification plate had been removed, presumably by some
souvenir hunter. There was a coronet at the head end of the coffin, from which six pearls were suspiciously absent. The lid was
loose; he dared to lift it and found a lead coffin which had been
torn open. Inside this he came to another wooden coffin, with a
lid that had never been nailed down. Fearing the worst, that
Byron himself might have been removed, he lifted the final lid:
before his eyes 'lay the embalmed body of Byron in as perfect a
condition as when it was placed in the coffin 114 years ago. His
features and hair easily recognisable from portraits .. The serene,
almost happy expression on his face made a profound impression
on me. The feet and ankles were uncovered, and I was able to

establish the fact that his lameness had been that of the right foot.' (Portraits from the life, with the club foot concealed by foliage, are in agreement with this.)

Inscriptions: (near where the body lies, on a slab donated by the King of Greece, 1881) ND. (on the chancel wall) 'In the vault beneath, where many of his ancestors and his mother are buried, lie the remains of George Gordon Noel Byron, Lord Byron of Rochdale in the County of Lancaster, the author of Childe Harold's Pilgrimage. He ... engaged in the glorious attempt to restore (Greece) to her ancient freedom and renown.' (memorial in Westminster Abbey):
'But there is that within me which shall tire Torture and Time, and breathe when I expire.'

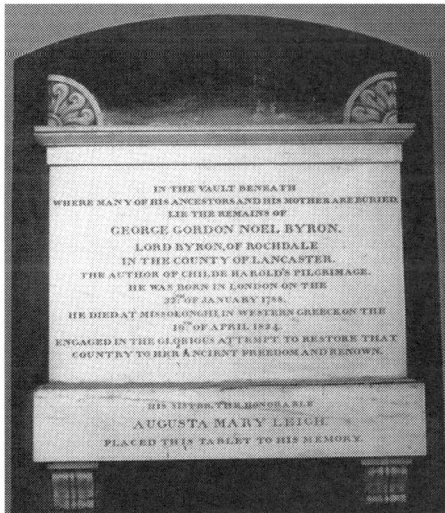

George Gordon, Lord Byron,
Cared not for the ozone and kept the fire on.
Something young ladies generally learned
Only as their knickers burned.

THOMAS CAMPBELL

Died 1844, age 66. Buried Westminster Abbey, London. As his
health failed, he gave a farewell party for friends in London, then
retired to Boulogne to die 'in a change of air'. A Polish nobleman
threw soil from the grave of the Polish patriot, Košciusko,
onto his coffin.

Inscription: (his own verse)
'The spirit shall return to him
Who gave its heavenly spark,
Yet think not, sun, it shall be dim
When thou thyself art dark!
No! It shall live again and shine
In bliss unknown to beams of thine,
By Him recall'd to breath,
Who captive led captivity,
Who robb'd the grave of victory,
And took the sting from death.'

Why did Thomas Campbell
Funk any bet or gamble?
My guess, his wins had always been
'Like angel-visits, few and far between'.

THOMAS CAMPION

Died 1620, age 53, probably of the plague, over which being a
'doctor in phisicke' gave him no advantage; and also in poverty,
(left £23) despite having been the 'pop idol' of his generation.
Buried St Dunstan-in-the-West, Fleet Street, London, where you
would have to arrive on a Tuesday lunchtime and imagine him
under some part of the church which has been converted to suit
the Romanian Orthodox form of worship, with many impressive
icons. There is a plaque on the wall for one Giles Campion,
died 1697, age 50, which might be some indication
of the site of the burial.

Inscription: None.

**With 'Cherry-ripe!', Thomas Campion
Topped the pops as ballad champion.
But 'Oh, come quickly!' was no goer;
Normally lovers like it slower.**

THOMAS CHATTERTON

Died, starving, 1770, age 17. The coroner found he had committed suicide by taking arsenic, but there is a theory he mistakenly took an overdose of a remedy for syphilis, such as opium. Although he died with creditors owing him enough to pay for a decent funeral, he was buried in Shoe Lane workhouse burial ground (behind St Andrew's Church, Farringdon Street, City of London), but later removed, in a mass of paupers' bones, to the graveyard known as St George's Fields, at the end of Heathcote Street, off Gray's Inn Road.

Inscription: None.

**Mouth size was something Chatterton
Was flattered on.
Before he could be kissed
He'd swallow his fist.**

GEOFFREY CHAUCER

Died 1400, age about 57, possibly of the plague. Buried
Westminster Abbey, London (the first commoner to be interred
there and 'founder member' of Poets' Corner.)

*Inscription: (the original fifteenth century Latin inscription was
different from the present one and 'wreten on a table hongyng on
a pylere by his sepulture'): 'Galfridus Chaucer vates et fama
poesis maternae hac sacra sum tumulatus humo.' (current)
'Qui fuit Anglorum vates ter maximus olim Galfridus Chaucer
conditur hoc tumulo annum si quaeras Domini si tempora
mortis ecce notae subsunt qua tibi cuncta notant. Aerum
narum requies mors.'*

**Lust for the Wife of Bath made Chaucer
Want to force her,
But that sort of thing wasn't done
By poets in 1381.**

G(ilbert) K(eith) CHESTERTON

Died 1935, age 62. Buried Roman Catholic Cemetery, Shepherds
Lane, off Candlemas Lane, Beaconsfield, Buckinghamshire.
Likely to have set a record for the heaviest poetic load ever to
trouble pallbearers.

Inscription: '*Pray for the soul of Gilbert Keith Chesterton.
Termino Nobis Donet in Patria.*'

**G K Chesterton,
Weighed in his vest a ton.
He'd have needed a sturdy van to
Transport him to Lepanto.**

JOHN CLARE

Died 1864, age 70, in Northampton Lunatic Asylum, where he had been for many years, deluded that he was Byron or Napoleon, and believing in a bigamous marriage to a childhood sweetheart that had in fact never taken place. Gradually became infirm and died quietly. Buried in St Botolph's churchyard, Helpston, Cambridgeshire, a sparrow's flight from where he had been born.

Inscriptions: (on tombstone) 'Sacred to the memory of the Northamptonshire Peasant Poet, John Clare. A Poet is born not made.' (memorial in Westminster Abbey: 'Fields were the essence of the song.'

John Clare
Wasn't always all there.
When asked where he'd been,
'Nutting, with the Empress Josephine.'

SAMUEL TAYLOR COLERIDGE

Died 1834, age 61, at house of apothecary treating him for opium
addiction. Spent great part of last twelve years in bed. Post
mortem revealed no cause. During final illness asked his wife and
daughter not to visit him, to spare them distress. Wished to focus
his thoughts on redemption. Buried in the graveyard at High
Street, Highgate, London, in 1868 transferred to the crypt of
nearby St Michael's Church, central aisle, green stone slab.

Inscription: (self-composed)
'Stop, Christian passer-by!
Stop, Child of God! And read
with gentle breast. Beneath this
sod A poet lies, or that which
once seem'd he. O, lift one
thought in prayer for S.T.C.
That he who many a year with
toil of breath Found death in life,
may here find life in death!
Mercy for praise, to be forgiven
for fame, he ask'd, and hoped
through Christ. Do thou
the same!'

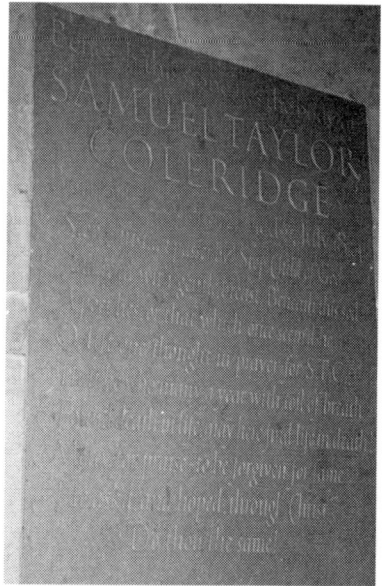

It made no difference to Coleridge,
Albatross, mole, pig-
Eon, trout: any time he bounced a cheque
He'd hang some creature round his neck!

WILLIAM COWPER

Died 1800, age 68, of dropsy, inconsolable after the loss of his dear companion, Mary Unwin. Buried in St Nicholas Church, East Dereham, Norfolk.

Inscription: *Rather than the ten lifeless lines inscribed on the actual tomb ('Pay your fond tribute to Cowper's dust!' etc.) I prefer the poet's own words, inscribed on the Cowper Memorial Church, Dereham, beginning 'I was a stricken deer, that left the herd long since, With many an arrow infix'd my panting side was charged.'*

**Bilious Cowper
Repudiated BUPA.
One of his dearest whims
Was therapy by hymns.**

GEORGE CRABBE

Died 1832, age 77, after gradual decline during which he suffered from a painful facial tic. Buried St James's Church, Trowbridge, Wiltshire, in chancel, with marble memorial on wall above, depicting him on deathbed with ministering angels and a communion cup illuminated by rays of light.

Inscription: 'Born in humble life, he made himself what he was; breaking through the obscurity of his birth by the force of his genius; yet he never ceased to feel for the less fortunate, entering, as his works can testify, into the sorrows and wants of the poorest of his parishioners, and so discharging the duties of a pastor and a magistrate as to endear himself to all around him. As a writer he cannot be better described than in the words of a great poet,* "Tho' Nature's sternest painter, yet her best."' (* Byron)

**For his supper, George Crabbe
Made do with a dab,
Whilst praying to God
He should marry and have cod.**

W(illiam) H(enry) DAVIES

Died 1940, age 69. Cremated and ashes scattered at Cheltenham Cemetery. Today's molehills in the Garden of Remembrance might have been an inspiration to his muse. Osbert Sitwell records that Mrs Davies told him three months before her husband's death, 'that his heart showed alarming symptoms of weakness, and the doctors attributed its condition to the continual dragging weight of his wooden leg.' Davies himself told Sitwell he'd never been ill before, except when he lost a foot (train-jumping in hobo style while on his way to the Klondike, which led to the loss of a lower leg, as related in his Autobiography of a Super-Tramp), but now 'Sometimes I feel I should like to turn over on my side and die.'

Inscription: None.

**W H Davies
Adulated gravies,
But restaurant cars, for bad behaviour,
Denied him victuals that were gravier.**

CECIL DAY-LEWIS

Died 1972, age 68. Buried St Michael's churchyard, Stinsford, Nr. Dorchester, Dorset (according to his wish, as close as possible to the grave of his hero, Thomas Hardy.)

Inscription: (his own verse) 'Poet Laureate. Shall I be gone long? For ever and a day. To whom there belong? Ask the stone to say. Ask my song.'

A sigh from C. Day-Lewis:
'What I most rue is,
They didn't name a plant after me, like the freesia.
People would so have loved the seedaylewisia!'

WALTER DE LA MARE

Died 1956, age 83. Ashes buried St Paul's Cathedral, London; commemorative plaque in the crypt. Death mask in the National Portrait Gallery, London. During an earlier flirtation with the Grim Reaper (1928), a visitor asked De la Mare whether he would like fruit or flowers. The weak reply, 'No, my dear; too late for fruit, too soon for flowers.'

Inscription: *'One-time choirboy of St Paul's. Where blooms the flower when her petals fade, Where sleepeth echo by earth's music made, Where all things transient to the changeless win, There waits the peace thy spirit dwelleth in.'*

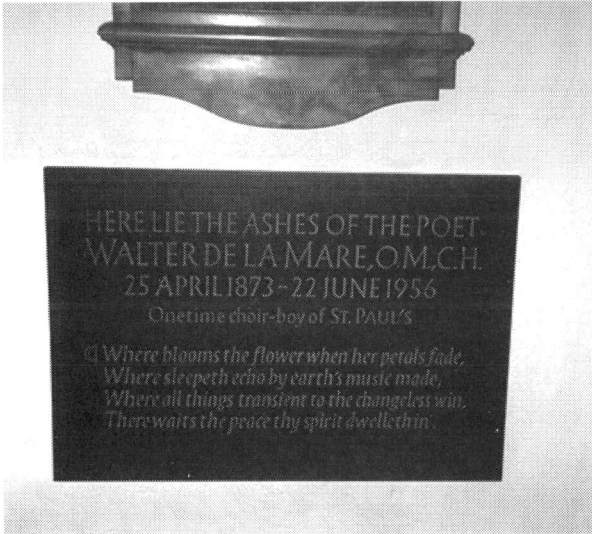

**Many a day did Walter De la Mare
Lounge in a British Museum chair
And ask the librarian, with casual air,
'Have you got *The Listener* there?'**

JOHN DONNE

Died 1631, age 59. Buried 'Old' St Paul's Cathedral, London. Monument, the only one to survive the Great Fire, 1666, now in the south choir aisle of the 'New' Cathedral. Well before his death he posed naked in his winding sheet for a painting to be made for his monument, then afterwards slept with the painting beside his bed. His ambition to die in the pulpit of St Paul's was not fulfilled. Delivered his last sermon, Death's Duel, retired to bed, but took five weeks to complete his exit. Carefully laid himself out and closed his own eyes before drawing his last breath.

Inscription: Johannes Donne sac theol profess poet varia studia quibus ab annis tenerrimus fideliter nec infeliciter incubuit instinctu et impulse spir scti monttu et hortatu regis iacobi anno sui iesu 1614 et suae aetat 42 decanatu huius eccles indutus 27th novemb 1621 exutus morte ultima die martii Ao 1631 hic licet in occiduo cinere aspicit eum cuius nomen est oriens. (Poetic licence allows us to add: 'Never send to know for whom the bell tolls; it tolls for thee.')

**For Donne
The apogee of fun
Was preaching to a flea
On the text of Job, chapter 23.**

MICHAEL DRAYTON

Died 1631, age 67 or 68. Buried Westminster Abbey,
London (in the north aisle.)

*Epitaph: (ascribed to Ben Jonson) 'A memorable poet of this
age, Exchanged his laurell for a crowne of glorye. Doe, pious
marble, let thy Readers knowe, What they and what their children
owe To Draiton's name; whose sacred dust Wee recommend unto
thy trust; Protect his mem'ry, and preserve his storye, Remain a
lasting monument of his Glorye, And when the Ruines shall dis-
clame To be the Treas'rer of his name, His name, that cannot
fade, shall be An everlasting Monument to Thee.'*

**The birth of the ode was something Drayton
Could put a date on.
Since when, down to the time of ice cream sodas,
There have been many bad odours.**

JOHN DRYDEN

Died 1700, age 68 'under the most excruciating of dolours'. After being confined with gout, got gangrene in a toe and refused to have it amputated. Buried Westminster Abbey, London. Died in poverty, after losing the Laureateship in 1688 for refusal to take Oath of Uniformity. Dr Johnson tells an extraordinary tale of the funeral, but stops short of vouching for its accuracy: Two peers had stumped up £540 for an Abbey burial; the cortege, with eighteen coachloads of mourners, was waylaid by some drunken rakes led by Lord Jefferies who made a better offer (£1,000). This was to include embalming, but, despite hot weather, the undertaker didn't carry this out, because Lord Jefferies reneged on the whole deal. The corpse, now 'very offensive', was removed to the College of Physicians, where a third attempt was made to arrange a suitable funeral, this time by subscription. About one subscriber Pope quipped, 'He helped to bury whom he helped to starve.' The burial finally took place three weeks after the death. Before setting out for the Abbey, a friend preached a Latin oration over the corpse, standing on a beer barrel, the lid of which gave way, so that the speech ended with the orator in the barrel. The interment, in the same grave as Chaucer, attracted so many sightseers that only those with drawn swords got near enough to see it. Afterwards Lord Jefferies was challenged to a duel over his misconduct, but refused to answer.

Inscription: ND

**Scholars of Dryden
We are rash to confide in.
One confused his *Absalom and Achitophel*
With Marquis's *Archy and Mehitabel.***

J.DRYDEN.

Natus 1632. Mortuus Maij 1 1700.

JOANNES SHEFFIELD DUX BUC-
KINGHAMIENSIS POSUIT. 1720.

STEPHEN DUCK

Died 1756, age 51, at Reading. 'Falling at length into a low-spirited melancholy way he grew lunatic and in a fit of that disorder threw himself from a bridge into the Thames.' (Encyclopaedia Britannica, 1766.) This would have to be the old Caversham Bridge pictured opposite. A later version has it that the act took place 'in a trout stream running behind the Black Lion Inn' (Duck's 'silver Kennet') but this lacked a bridge. There is no extant Black Lion, but in 1823 one stood on the corner of Broad Street and West Street, between the two rivers. There is no record of Duck's burial, either at Reading, where he died, at Byfleet, his last place of residence as rector, or at his birthplace, Charlton St Peter, in Wiltshire. It was customary to bury suicides at dead at night, without any formality, and in unconsecrated ground often at a crossroads, with a stake through the heart.

Duck started out as a thresher ('No intermission in our work we know, The noisy threshal must for ever go'), but after marrying Queen Caroline's housekeeper, according to Dr Johnson, was patronised by the Queen 'with uncommon ardour' and made first a Yeoman of the Guard and then her librarian.

Memorial: Duck has none except that a 'Threshers' Feast' or 'Duck Feast' has been held in his honour at Charlton St Peter, on 1 June continuously since 1735. No other English poet has such a remembrance.

'Duck,'
Cried Her Majesty, 'What blessed luck!
Two grisly fates you've missed
The Laureateship, *and* the Faber list!'

Old Caversham Bridge

T(homas) S(tearns) ELIOT

Died 1965, age 76. Ashes buried in St Michael's Church, East
Coker, Nr. Yeovil, Somerset, where there is a tablet set in the rear
wall.

Inscriptions: (at East Coker, including lines from Four Quartets)
'Of your charity pray for the repose of the soul of (ND). In my
beginning is my end, in my end is my beginning.' (on memorial in
Westminster Abbey) 'The communication of the dead is tongued
with fire beyond the language of the living.'

The cats kept by Eliot
Were an awfully smelly lot.
They crapped a lot and were not chaste;
No wonder the land was waste.

EDWARD FITZGERALD

Died 1883, age 74, in his sleep while on annual visit to a friend at Merton, Norfolk. Wished to be cremated, but the first British crematorium was not yet in use. Buried St Michael's churchyard, Boulge, Nr. Bredfield, Suffolk, in open ground rather than in the nearby family vault, because he 'wished to hear the songs of birds'. By his grave is a rose bush raised from seed collected from a rose that grows on Omar Khayyam's own grave at Naishapur, Iran, and planted by the Omar Khayyam Club in 1893.

Inscription: 'It is He that hath made us, and not we ourselves.'

**The fair sex, FitzGerald
Never imperilled.
As for song and wine,
He'd always decline.**

JAMES ELROY FLECKER

Died of consumption, 1915, age 30. Buried Cheltenham Cemetery, Gloucestershire, almost the first grave past the entrance. On the Cemetery's list of 'famous ones', along with an Australian explorer, an antiques dealer, a jockey who won the Grand National five times, and one of the Rolling Stones. Passed away in a sanatorium (his 'mattrass grave') at Davos, Switzerland, of disease contracted in Constantinople. Frank Savery: 'He was very cheerful that spring (of 1914)... I saw him once more, in December... already visibly dying,... he was determined to do two things: to complete his poem, The Burial in England, and to put his business affairs into the hands of a competent literary agent.' With passenger sailings disrupted by war, Flecker's body was brought home on a British destroyer.

Inscription: 'O Lord, restore his realm to the dreamer.'

**Not at all cut out was Roy Flecker
For Chancellor of the Exchequer.
Money matters may not busy us
If we think we are Odysseus.**

JOHN GAY

Died 1732, age 47, after a violent fit. Buried Westminster Abbey, London (monument in triforium and inaccessible to public.)

Inscriptions: (his own epitaph)
'Life is a jest,
and all things show it;
I thought so once,
and now I know it.'
(and by Pope)
'Of manners gentle,
of affections mild;
In wit a man;
simplicity a child;
With native humour
temp'ring virtuous rage,
Form'd to delight at once
and lash the age;
Above temptation,
in a low estate,
And uncorrupted,
e'en among the great;
A safe companion,
and an easy friend,
Unblam'd thro' life,
lamented in thy end,
These are thy honours!
not that here thy bust
Is mix'd with heroes,
or with kings thy dust;
But that the worthy
and the good shall say,
Striking their pensive bosoms -
here lies GAY.'

**From up above, Gay
Complained that his play
Had been wrecked
By Brecht.**

OLIVER GOLDSMITH

Died of fever, 1774, age 44. Doctored himself with James's Powder, contrary to his apothecary's advice. Plan to bury him in Westminster Abbey aborted by his debts. Instead buried Temple Church, Fleet Street, London. A stone on the north side, marking his burial place, was demolished in the Blitz. Asked on his deathbed if his mind was at ease, replied, 'No, it is not.'

Inscription*: (In expectation of Goldsmith's burial in Westminster Abbey, Samuel Johnson prepared this Latin epitaph, declaring English would disgrace the holy place. In the end, it got to Poets' Corner, but the poet didn't.) 'Poetae, Physici, Historici qui nullum fere scribendi genus non tetigit, nullum quod tetigit non ornavit, sive risus essent movendi, sive lacrimae, affectuum potens, at lenis dominator, ingenio sublimis, vividus, versatilis, oratione grandis, nitidus, venustus Hoc monumento memoriam coluit. Sodalium amor, Amicorum fides, Lectorem veneratio.' In private, Johnson declared, 'No man was more foolish when he had not a pen in his hand or more wise when he had.'*

About Oliver Goldsmith
They tell a quaint old myth
That (because he often did it) he was fond
Of falling in a pond.

THOMAS GRAY

Died 1771, age 54, at Pembroke Hall, Cambridge. Had been in poor health for some time and finally died of gout of the stomach. His last words, to a cousin: 'Molly, I shall die.' Buried St Giles's churchyard, Stoke Poges, Buckinghamshire. A monument with quotations from the famous Elegy is set in a nearby field where it is supposed to have been composed..

Inscription: (on the adjacent church wall) 'Opposite to this stone in the same tomb upon which he has so feelingly recorded his grief at the loss of a beloved parent are deposited the remains of Thomas Gray, the author of the Elegy in a Country Churchyard.'

**There's a file on Thomas Gray
At the RSPCA.
You can't complain about that
If you claim a goldfish killed a cat.**

IVOR GURNEY

Died 1937, age 47, of pulmonary tuberculosis. Buried St Matthew's churchyard, Twigworth, Gloucestershire. His nervous frailty was aggravated by shellshock on the Western Front in World War I, and he was committed in 1922 to the City of London Mental Hospital, Dartford, Kent, where he ended his days.The composer Gerald Finzi described the funeral as a 'sad little affair' where Gurney's lifelong friend, Herbert Howells, 'played *Sleep* and *Seven Meadows* on a wheezy little organ.' The present headstone replaced, in 2000, an earlier cross of crusty-looking stone, with leaded lettering.

Inscription: (formerly) 'To the memory of Ivor Gurney, musician and poet, a lover and maker of beauty. Inside the waters of comfort.' (now) 'Composer. Poet of the Severn and the Somme.'

**Ivor Gurney
Could have used a 'present from Ernie'.
It's easy for a genius
Living on buns to become neurasthenious.**

THOMAS HARDY

Died 1928, age 87, three weeks before the first performance of Gustav Holst's Egdon Heath, which he had been waiting to hear. Buried Westminster Abbey, London (body) and St Michael's churchyard, Stinsford, Nr Dorchester, Dorset (heart.) Wished to be buried intact in his native county, but arrangements for him to join Poets' Corner were in train before the family realised. His heart is said to have been transported to Dorset in a biscuit tin, and en route was possibly chewed by his pet cat.

Inscriptions: (Stinsford) 'Here lies the heart of Thomas Hardy, OM. His ashes are buried in Westminster Abbey.' (Abbey) ND.

Thomas Hardy
Agitated the Mahdi,
Who said, 'One tenet we must part on –
There've got to be camels in that barton!'

W(illiam) E(rnest) HENLEY

Died 1903, age 53, never fully recovered (so much for Invictus!) from the shock of an accident sustained when he alighted from a moving railway carriage. He landed on the artifical limb that replaced the foot he lost when a child due to tubercular infection. Cremated at Woking, Surrey, ashes buried St John the Baptist's churchyard, Cockayne Hatley, Bedfordshire.

Inscription: *(the final stanza of his Margaritæ Sorori):*

'So be my passing!
My task accomplish'd
and the long day done,
My wages taken,
and in my heart
Some late lark singing,
Let me be gather'd
to the quiet West,
The sundown splendid
and serene, Death.'

W E Henley
Urged men to be more menly.
I too could be master of my fate
If it allowed me to get up late.

GEORGE HERBERT

Died 1633, age 39, of consumption. Buried St Andrew's Church,
Lower Bemerton, Wiltshire, under the chancel floor. Aubrey
describes his tomb, 'Under no large, nor yet very good, marble
gravestone, without any inscription.' Today you will find a small
tablet, inscribed 'G.M. 1632', set in the wall to the side of the
altar; it looks original, and resembles other typical markers of the
age set in the floor. On his deathbed asked a friend to publish his
poems only if they might benefit 'any dejected poor soul'.
Choristers from Salisbury Cathedral sang at his funeral. At the
west end of the church is a more modern memorial stained glass
window, depicting the poet holding a violin.

Inscription: Initials and year
(according to old style calendar).

Exposed to the female gaze, Herbert
Fizzed like sherbet.
But it's not to some girls' taste
To squeeze a man who's like toothpaste.

ROBERT HERRICK

Died 1674, age 83. Buried St George the Martyr's churchyard, Dean Prior, Devon. Grave unmarked and whereabouts unknown. This may be the result of rejection by his parishioners with whom he was continually at odds. He once threw his sermon at an inattentive congregation. Wherever he lies, his bones will be rattled by the incessant traffic on the A38 expressway which must pass almost above his nose.

Memorial: His name is in the stained glass window above Poets' Corner, Westminster Abbey.

Too rash and choleric was Herrick
To be a cleric.
If a priest *must* swear, Heaven
Prefers a 'Bloody Hell!' to 'Bloody Devon!'

THOMAS HOOD

Died 1845, age 45, of rheumatic heart disease and overwork on his magazine, spending his last five months in bed. Had previously secured an advance from his publisher by mortgaging his brain. Buried Kensal Green Cemetery, London. A poem in Punch by Eliza Cook, 1852, remarked on the shameful lack of any monument, while neighbouring graves of a 'circus hero' and a horse trainer had 'gorgeous cenotaphs'. A public subscription was at once raised and a monument erected, with bas-reliefs depicting Eugene Aram's Dream and the Bridge of Sighs, and a fine monumental bust, but these were stolen and only the pedestal remains.

Inscription: 'He sang the Song of the Shirt.'

**Tom Hood
Liked girls that were good,
But if they were given to vice
Also found them nice.**

GERARD MANLEY HOPKINS

Died of typhoid fever, 1889, age 44. Buried Glasnevin Cemetery, Finglas Road, Dublin, Ireland (in an unmarked grave in the Jesuits' common plot, to the left of the entrance.) At the time of his death, Hopkins regarded himself as an exile, sent by the Society of Jesus to teach Classics to unresponsive college students. Conscientious marking of exam scripts worsened his neurosis. There is a memorial stone in Westminster Abbey.

Inscription: (on Jesuit memorial at Glasnevin) ND (on monument in Westminster Abbey) 'Immortal diamond.'

**Gerard Manley Hopkins
Often had gory chopkins,
For as he shaved, there was sung
Plain song with the rhythms sprung.**

A(lfred) E(dward) HOUSMAN

Died 1936, age 77, in a nursing home in Cambridge. Ashes buried St Lawrence's churchyard, Ludlow, Shropshire (beneath the north wall.) When on his deathbed his doctor told him a dirty joke, he responded, 'That's a good one. Tomorrow I'll tell it on the Golden Floor.'

Inscription: (on small tablet covering the deposit) 'Hic jacet A. E. H.' (on the wall above) 'In Memory of Alfred Edward Housman, MA Oxon, Kennedy Professor of Latin and Fellow of Trinity College, University of Cambridge, Author of The Shropshire Lad ... Goodnight ensured release, Imperishable peace: Have these for yours.'

**On hilltops the Shropshire Lad
Sat when his piles were not so bad.
Any other time, he sat in
A comfortable chair of Latin.**

TED HUGHES

Died 1998, age 68, of a heart attack, in London Bridge Hospital,
where he'd been having treatment for colonic cancer.
Funeral held at St Peter's church, North Tawton, Devon,
with many university friends present, after which he
was cremated at Exeter. One of his poems was read
by Seamus Heaney.
At the memorial service in Westminster Abbey the recorded
voice of Hughes recited Shakespeare's 'Fear no more the heat
of the sun.' Poet Laureate, 1984 -98.

*We have been informed that there is no stone or memorial for
Ted Hughes in the churchyard at North Tawton.*

**Ted Hughes
One would never accuse
Of a mouth that was mealy.
· No one mistook him for the Bishop of Ely.**

BEN JONSON

Died 1637, age 65. In his later years suffered from palsy and paralysis. Buried Westminster Abbey, London (north aisle of the nave.) Told that burial space there was at a premium, he suggested he should be buried upright (so as to occupy only two foot by two foot of horizontal space) and this was granted.

Inscription: An H introduced into his name by a mason while renewing it. Contains a pun : 'O rare Ben Jonson' can be read as eulogy or invocation (orare = pray for).

They scoffed at Jonson:
'For you, eye-contact just isn't on, son!
With one orb lower than its mate
Your only chance is on Blind Date!'

JOHN KEATS

Died of consumption, 1821, age 25. Buried Cimitero degli Inglesi, Rome, Italy. He believed unrequited love to be the true cause of his mortal sickness. Research concludes he was infected with tuberculosis whilst caring for his younger brother, Tom (d.1818), and that inappropriate use of mercury to cure syphilis possibly hastened his death. On his deathbed was obsessed with these words from the Beaumont and Fletcher play, Philaster:
' ... all your better deeds Shall be in water writ.'

Inscription: (under a lyre with a broken string) 'This Grave contains all that was Mortal, of a YOUNG ENGLISH POET Who, on his Death Bed, in the Bitterness of his Heart at the Malicious Power of his Enemies, Desired these Words to be engraven on his Tomb Stone: Here lies One whose Name was writ in Water.'

**Calling himself Steak was one of Keats'
Conceits.
Asked to explain this stunt,
Said, 'Truth is Beauty only back to front.'**

RUDYARD KIPLING

Died 1936, in hospital after an operation, age 70. Asked by his doctor what was wrong with him, said 'Something's come loose inside.' It was haemorrhage from a perforated duodenum. Ashes buried in Westminster Abbey, after cremation at Golders Green Cemetery, North London.

Inscription: ND

**Who'd believe Kipling
Hadn't been tippling,
When he referred to the lav
As the Rikki-Tikki-Tav?**

PHILIP LARKIN

Died in hospital 1985, age 63, following surgery to remove his cancerous oesophagus. During the operation further inoperable tumours came to light, but he wasn't told of these, because of his fear of death. 'I don't think about death *all* the time, though I don't see why I shouldn't...Why aren't I screaming?' he wrote to John Wain, shortly before his final illness. Final words to the nurse, 'I am going to the inevitable'. Funeral at St Mary the Virgin, Cottingham, Humberside. Buried Cottingham Cemetery, (in the eighth row beyond the garden of remembrance reserved for cremations, to the left of the main entrance.)

Inscription: After the name and dates, just the one word 'Writer'.

Librarian Larkin
Wore clothes I wouldn't be seen in the dark in,
But dare one expect a suit that fits
From a man with five D. Litts.?

D(avid) H(erbert) LAWRENCE

Died 1930, age 44, in a sanatorium at Vence, near Nice, France, of pulmonary tuberculosis. Cremated and ashes mixed into masonry of the altar in his personal crypt at San Cristobal, Taos County, New Mexico, USA. It is apt to be festooned with condoms. His name was also added to the family monument in the cemetery at Eastwood, Nottinghamshire, where he was born.

Inscriptions: (at Eastwood) 'Unconquered.' (on monument in Westminster Abbey) 'Homo sum! the adventurer.'

**'If the condom,' said Lawrence,
'Was an abhorrence,
I'd have written more prissily
About the serpents of Sicily.'**

ANDREW MARVELL

Died suddenly 1678, age 57, from a tertian fever, 'through the ignorance of an old conceited doctor. An ounce of Peruvian bark' (quinine?) 'would have saved him, but instead he was given an opiate, and copiously bled.' The rumour that he was poisoned by Jesuits seems malicious. Buried St Giles-in-the-Fields Church, St Giles High Street, Bloomsbury, London, traditionally under the pews in the middle of the south aisle. The Oxford Literary Guide to the British Isles (1977) mentions a memorial on the north wall of the church, but there is nothing to be seen today.

Inscription: None.

**The problem for Marvell,
His member was larval.
His mistress coy? Nothing would sate her
But the most ingenious vibrator!**

JOHN MASEFIELD

Died at his home near Abingdon, Oxfordshire, 1967, age 88.
Buried Westminster Abbey, London. The memorial plaque
depicted is in the church at Preston, Nr. Ledbury, Herefordshire.
Poet Laureate, 1930-67.

Inscription: ND

On the deck stood John Masefield
With salt-caked supper half-congealed:
'I find my tummy is a heaver,
Quite unadapted to sea fever!'

GEORGE MEREDITH

Died quietly, after catching a chill, 1909, age 81. Previously
crippled by paraplegia. After cremation, ashes laid as he wished
next to his wife in Dorking Cemetery, Dorking, Surrey; a
splendid back-drop of Box Hill, which he had been in the habit of
climbing every morning. The grave (number 4219 in plot P, close
to the Anglican Chapel) consists of a stone like an open book and
some kerbing. Was refused burial in Westminster Abbey because
of his freethinking views (his school in Germany instilled in boys
a republican spirit, love of nature, and faith in the brotherhood of
man.) At the funeral, his son bore his Order of Merit on a cushion
of wild daisies. A memorial service was held the same day in
Westminster Abbey, with Hardy, Kipling, and Henry James
attending. J M Barrie wrote a description of the funeral day.

*Inscription: (a quotation from his novel, Vittoria): 'Life is but a
little holding Lent to do a nightly labour.'*

**Said his wife, 'Mr Meredith
I'd rather not be buried with.
It's always been such a nuisance,
His banging on about translucence!'**

JOHN MILTON

Died, 'by a quiet and silent expiration', from 'gout struck in', 1674, age 65. Buried St Giles, Cripplegate, London (near the pulpit, and next to his father). (Best approach: from Moorgate tube station, then via Fore St.) The funeral 'was very splendidly and numerously attended.' During repairs to the church, 1790, his coffin was unearthed. There is a contemporary record of the vandalisation that followed: a publican 'pulled hard at the teeth, which resisted until someone hit them a knock with a stone.' A pawnbroker 'took a large quantity of Milton's hair'.
After this, the parish gravedigger (a lady) exhibited the remains at sixpence a peep. There is a full length statue in St Giles.

Inscriptions: (on the grave) 'Near to this spot is buried John Milton, Author of Paradise Lost.' (on the statue's plinth, quoting Paradise Lost): ' ... may (the Poet) assert Eternal Providence, and justify the wayes of God to man.'

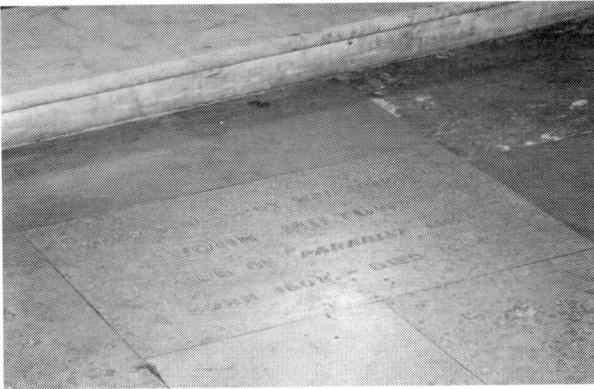

**Very fond was Milton
Of inquiries about land to be built on,
Debates he would often fuel
With ideas for paradise renewal.**

THOMAS MOORE

Died 1852, age 72. In 1849 he'd been seized with a fit, after
which he lost his memory almost completely. Buried St
Nicholas's churchyard, Bromham, Wiltshire, under a Celtic cross
so huge as to be totally unimpressive - all of fifteen foot! Stained
glass window in his memory at the western end of the church.
Not exactly an epitaph, but William Hazlitt passed judgement on
Moore's folksy Irish Melodies, saying he had 'converted the wild
harp of Erin into a musical snuff-box.'

Inscription:

'Dear harp of my country!
In darkness I found thee.
The cold chain of silence
Had hung o'er thee long,
When proudly,
my own island's harp!
I unbound thee
And gave all thy chords
To light, freedom and song.'

Ever the patriot, Tom Moore
Was partial to an Irish snore.
Noises that issued from his hooter
Reminded one of Phil the Fluter!

WILFRED OWEN

Killed in action, 1918, age 25, while crossing the Sambre and Oise Canal. Buried Ors Communal Cemetery (N.B. not Ors British Cemetery), Nord, France, Row A, Grave 3. The cemetery is north-west of Ors, a village between Le Cateau and Landrecies.

Inscription: In addition to name, rank, decoration (MC) and dates, the headstone bears these lines: 'Shall life renew These bodies? Of a truth All death will he annul.'

**Out of poor Wilfred Owen
Poppies started growin'
Just a week before
The end of the war.**

SYLVIA PLATH

Died by gassing herself in her London flat, 1963, age 31. Buried St Thomas's churchyard, Heptonstall, Hebden Bridge, West Yorkshire. This well-known quote from her poem Lady Lazarus is sometimes construed as a prediction: 'Dying Is an art like everything else.'

Inscription: *'Even amidst fierce flames The golden lotus can be planted.'*

**Ms. Plath
Was no polymath.
One big bee Sylvia had
In her bonnet: that was Dad.**

ALEXANDER POPE

Died quietly 1744, age 56, after five years' affliction with asthma. Nearing death, suffered from the delusion of an arm coming out of a wall. Sent for a priest to give him absolution. Buried St Mary the Virgin's Church, Twickenham, Middlesex (grave, between that of the Countess of Drogheda and the mayoral pew, formerly marked with a capital P, but since 1962 with a brass plate). Monument in north gallery. Skull dug up by phrenologists, since when his ghost is reputed to 'keep a low profile in the south gallery'. Wrote two epitaphs for himself; the better one is on his monument, which also cocks a snoot at Westminster Abbey, which would have refused him burial if it had been applied for, because he was a Catholic.

Inscriptions: (over grave)
'Here are buried the mortal remains
of Alexander Pope. Qui nil molitur
inepte. This tablet was placed by three
members of the Faculty of English of
Yale University 1962.' (in gallery)
'Poeta Loquitur. Heroes and Kings,
your distance keep: In peace let one poor
Poet sleep, Who never flatter'd Folks like
you! Let Horace blush, and Virgil too.
One who would not be buried in
Westminster Abbey.'

Alexander Pope
Sucked soap.
This accounts for the runs he had
While writing The Dunciad.

CHRISTINA ROSSETTI

Died 1894, of cancer, age 64. Buried Highgate Cemetery (older western section), North London. Painful disfiguring Graves' disease had been diagnosed in 1870. Screamed unaccountably every night for weeks before her death. Those hoping to see the grave should note it is not on the official tour route and special arrangements have to be made to see it. Christina shares a tomb with her brother Dante Gabriel and other members of the Rossetti family up to the present day. She herself is commemorated on a flat stone at the foot of the cross which records Dante Gabriel.

Inscription: There appear to be four lines of verse after her name and dates, but in present conditions these are not decipherable.

Christina Rossetti
Pronounced 'pretty' as 'pretti',
And the way she said 'Raphael'
One might think over-careful.

SIEGFRIED SASSOON

Died 1967, age 80. Buried St Andrew's churchyard, Mells, Nr. Frome, Somerset, fulfilling his wish to be as close as possible to Catholic priest and Bible translator, Ronald Knox. (Sassoon is in fact three rows closer to the church.) War poems in World War I made his name, but further notoriety came when, after decoration for courage in Flanders, he published a refusal to continue fighting and narrowly escaped court martial. Several autobiographical works, including Memoirs of a Fox-Hunting Man.

Inscription: ND + RIP (N.B. but not MC.)

'Tallyho!' sang Sassoon,
'I'm over the moon!'
'Then you're well out of bounds!'
Groused the Master of Hounds.

WILL SHAKSPER aka William Shakespeare

Died 1616, age 52. Buried Holy Trinity Church, Stratford-upon-Avon, Warwickshire. An almost contemporary vicar of Stratford-on-Avon states, 'Shakespear, Drayton and Ben Jhonson had a merry meeting and, itt seems, drank too hard, for Shakespear died of a feavour there contracted.' Made a will which he was doubt-fully able to sign, leaving among his effects more than one bed, but no books or manuscripts.

Inscription: (on tombstone)

GOOD FREND FOR IESVS SAKE FORBEARE,
TO DIGG THE DVST ENCLOASED HEARE:
BLESE BE Y MAN Y SPARES THES STONES,
AND CVRST BE HE Y MOVES MY BONES.

To move the bones could be hard work as it is recorded they lie seventeen feet down!

'What name shall I put? Shaksper?
Shakespeare?
Marlowe? Bacon? Perhaps de Vere?'
He always came over queer
When they said, 'Sign here.'

Other candidates for authorship of the Works of Shakespeare: Francis Bacon, d. 1616, age 65, caught cold during an experiment on preserving chicken by stuffing it with snow; Edward de Vere, Earl of Oxford, d. of plague, 1604, age 54; Christopher Marlowe, d. 1593, age 29, either murdered in a brawl or assassinated by secret agents.

The original monument to Shakespeare in Stratford-upon-Avon church (dating from before 1623) seems to have looked like this:

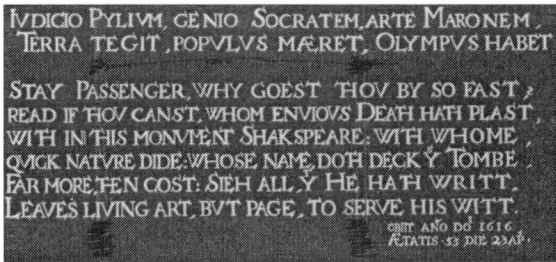

The first, Latin lines of the inscription mean 'A Nestor in judgement, a Socrates in genius, a Virgil in art. The earth covers him up, the people mourn him, and Olympus has him.' The inscription is of course incorrect in saying that he is buried 'within the monument'.

PERCY BYSSHE SHELLEY

Drowned near Livorno, Italy, 1822, age 29. Washed ashore, given temporary burial in the sands, then exhumed and cremated on the beach. Trelawney snatched from the pyre what he took to be the heart (more likely the liver), gave it to Mary Shelley, the poet's widow, who kept it (flat in a copy of *Adonis*) until her own death. It was buried with her in St Peter's churchyard, Bournemouth, Dorset. Shelley's ashes were interred in the Cimitero degli Inglesi, Rome, close to Keats. Trelawney describes finding the corpse: 'The face and hands, and parts of the body not protected by the dress, were fleshless. The tall slight figure, the jacket, the volume of Sophocles in one pocket, and Keats's poems in the other ... were all too familiar.' Shelley had written of 'hearing the sea Breathe o'er my dying brain its last monotony.'

Inscription (*from TheTempest*): *'Nothing of him that doth fade, But doth suffer a sea-change, Into something rich and strange.'*

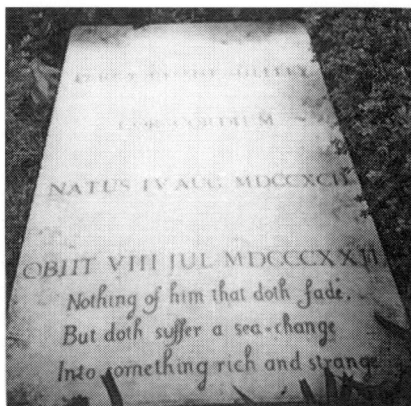

That visionary, P B Shelley,
Foresaw the telly.
His 'soap', in the style of Pindars,
Was to have been Westwinders.

SIR PHILIP SIDNEY

Died 1586, age 31, of a bullet wound in the thigh inflicted by a Spanish marksman during the Battle of Zutphen in the Netherlands. Buried crypt of 'Old' St Paul's Cathedral, London; lead coffin recognised 1667 after Great Fire and reinterred in the 'New' Cathedral, where there is a modern plaque in the crypt. There is the familiar story of how, as he lay dying, he chivalrously offered a 'common' soldier the drink of water that had been brought him, saying , "Thy need is greater than mine." Called for a favourite song to be sung as he lay dying.

Epitaph: His friend Fulke Greville wrote a poem 'Epitaph' for him, containing the line, 'Salute the stones, that keep the limbs, that held so good a mind.' This hagiography in spite of Philip's supposed incestuous relationship with his sister. **Inscription:** *'Poet Soldier Courtier and Diplomat + ND'*

Had Sir Philip Sidney
Been of a different kidney
He'd have kept that water to drink,
Given the dying man his ink.

JOHN SKELTON

Died 1529, age probably 69. Buried St Margaret's Church, Westminster, London; grave said to have been in the east end of the chancel, but nothing has survived restorations.

Inscription: (recorded as) 'Johannes Skeltonis, vates Pierius, hic situs est.'

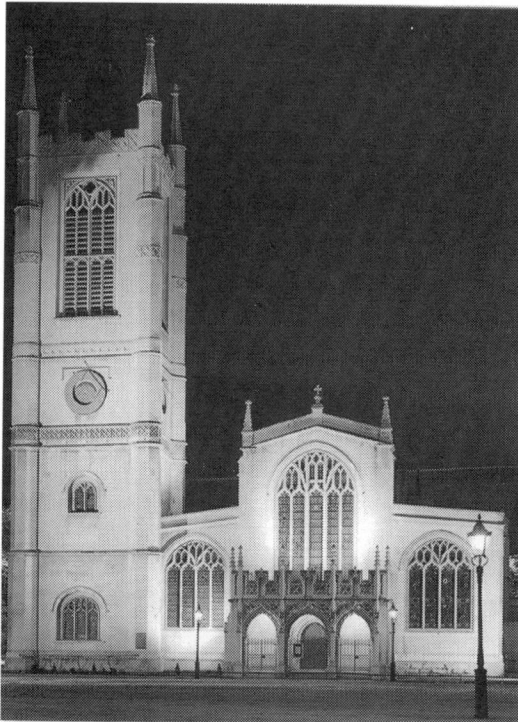

**In the presence of Skelton
People kept ear-muffs of felt on,
A defence against such doltery
As his imitations of poultry.**

ROBERT SOUTHEY

Died 1843, age 68. Death from fever and 'softening of the brain,' spelt out by the DNB: 'returned from his (second) wedding tour in a condition of utter mental exhaustion.... The last year of his life was a mere trance.' Buried St Kentigern's churchyard, Great Crosthwaite, Cumbria. The government of Brazil paid to restore his tomb in gratitude for his early history of that country. In The Scholar he expressed hopes that his name would 'not perish with the dust.'

Inscription: 'Here lies the body of Robert Southey, LLD, Poet Laureate (dates), for forty years a resident of this parish ... I am the resurrection and the life saith the Lord.'

**Thuffering from nuptial lithp, Thouthey
Called his thecond wife 'a huthy',
And began to abuthe her mightily
When Brathil's hithtory didn't amuthe her nightily.**

EDMUND SPENSER

Died 1599, age probably 47, in financial distress, at a lodging house in Westminster. As Sheriff of Cork, his health was undermined by the task of suppressing Irish 'troubles', during which Kilcolman Castle was burnt around him and one of his children killed. Buried Westminster Abbey, London, at the expense of the Earl of Essex, as Number Two in Poets' Corner. Camden reports, 'His hearse was attended by the gentlemen of his faculty, who cast into his tomb some funeral elegies, and the pens they were wrote with.'

Inscription: 'Heare lyes (expecting the Second Comminge of our Saviour Christ Jesus) the body of Edmond Spencer the Prince of Poets in his tyme whose divine spirrit needs noe othir witnesse then the works which he left behinde him.'

Nice to Elizabeth was Spenser,
***He* knew who was really censor.**
Urged the Thames to flow with power,
But not, we guess, towards the Tower.

ROBERT LOUIS STEVENSON

Died of apoplexy, 1894, age 44, at Vailima, Samoa, where he had settled for health reasons. Had declared: 'I wish to die in my boots, no more Land of Counterpane. If only I could secure a violent end, what a fine success! To be drowned, to be shot, to be thrown from a horse, aye, to be hanged, rather than pass again through that slow dissolution.' The grave is on the summit of Mount Veam, overlooking Vailima, and so difficult to reach that Laura Stubbs (Stevenson's Shrine, 1903) reports sixty Samoan bearers were needed to hack through forest and haul the coffin to the top. Local chiefs tabooed use of firearms so that birds may nest in peace near the tomb.

Inscription: (on one side of the sarcophagus, ND and his own verse) 'Under the wide and starry sky, Dig the grave and let me lie, Glad did I live and gladly die, And I lay me down with a will. This be the verse you grave for me, Here he lies where he longed to be. Home is the sailor, home from the sea, And the hunter home from the hill.' *(on the other side, a Samoan inscription)*

**Kids' tastes? Something Stevenson
Claimed not to be at sixes and sevens on.
But we know one child who nurses
The wish it had been A Garden of *Curses!***

HENRY HOWARD, EARL OF SURREY

Executed outside the Tower of London, 1547, age about 30.
Buried first at All Hallows Church, Barking (by the Tower),
removed 1614 to St Michael's Church, Framlingham, Suffolk,
where in 1835 his body was discovered directly beneath his
effigy. The dying Henry VIII had listened to his detractors, who
charged him with falsifying his coat of arms and advising
his sister to become the king's mistress, so as to enhance his own
claims to the throne. It was Howard who developed the
'Shakespearean' sonnet.

Inscription: ND

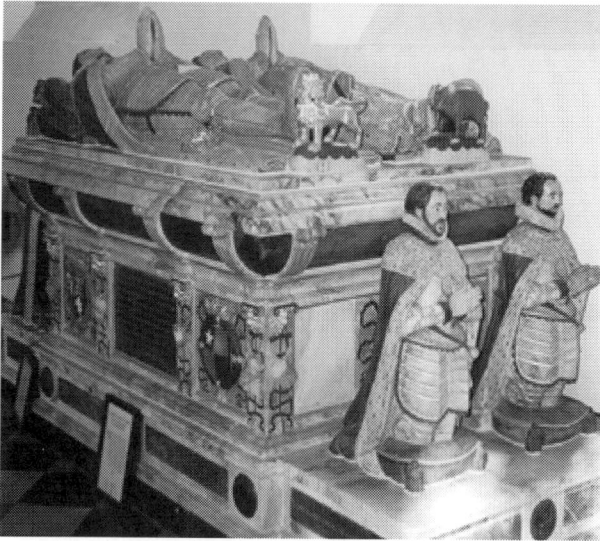

**Off to the scaffold, Howard
Was no coward,
But executed a sonnet
On it.**

ALGERNON CHARLES SWINBURNE

Died of pneumonia, 1909, age 72. Did well to fulfil his life
expectancy, as at his birth he was given only an hour to live.
Buried St Boniface's churchyard, Bonchurch, Isle of Wight.
Wished to be buried by his friends without any religious
ceremony, but an interfering priest insisted on reciting a
prayer over him.

Inscription: ND

**A warning: Swinburnia
Can give you a hernia.
Rhymes like 'glories' with 'sighs'
May damage your eyes.**

ALFRED LORD TENNYSON

Died 1892, age 83, having lost consciousness after an attack of influenza. Buried Westminster Abbey, London. After an earlier illness (rheumatic gout, 1889) he composed Crossing the Bar while on the ferry from Portsmouth to the Isle of Wight, and gave it to his nurse, who was shocked because it seemed to her like his own death song, with lines such as: 'May there be no moaning at the bar, When I put out to sea.'

Inscription: ND

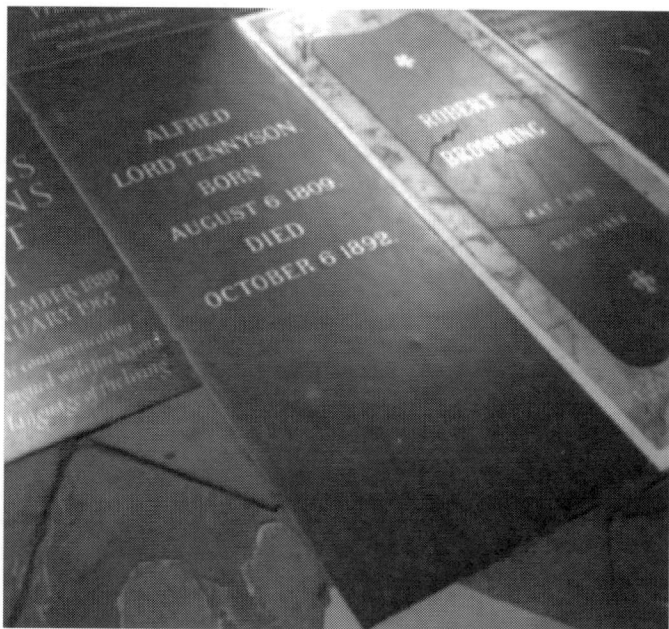

**The death of Arthur, Tennyson
Made millions of pennies on,
But Queen Victoria
Wished it were gorier.**

DYLAN THOMAS

Died 1953, age 39, on a reading tour in New York, USA, of alcohol poisoning. (After drinking eighteen straight whiskeys in a tavern, he fell into a six-day coma.) Buried St Martin's churchyard, Laugharne, Carmarthenshire. A short film clip of his funeral can be seen at the Dylan Thomas Centre, Swansea.

Inscriptions: (on grave) ND on white-painted wooden cross, with the same for his wife Caitlin on the reverse. (in Westminster Abbey) 'Time held me green and dying Though I sang in my chains like the sea.'

**Though Dylan Thomas
Vilified commerce,
He didn't damage the mystique
Of the Welsh love of leek.**

EDWARD THOMAS

Killed by exploding shell shortly after dawn on the snowy first day of the Arras offensive, 1917, age 39. Not far away from him, unknowing, was the novelist, Henry Williamson, who survived the attack. Thomas's daughter Myfanwy reported, 'His body was quite untouched but the war diary in his pocket bore strange seashell-like markings as though it had undergone tremendous and violent pressure.' Buried Agny Military Cemetery, Pas de Calais, France, Row C, Grave 43. Agny is just south of Achicourt, north-west of the main village across the River Crinchon, about 5 km from Arras railway station.

Inscription: Rank, name, regiment, date of death, age, nothing further.

**Imagine Edward Thomas
In the age of CD-Romers,
E.g. on his mobile at each stop:
'And now we're stuck in Adlestrop!'**

JAMES THOMSON

Died 1748, age 47. After a strenuous walk, caught a severe chill while being rowed from Hammersmith to Kew. Buried St Mary Magdalen's Church, Richmond, Surrey, 'under a plain stone near the font'. A memorial at the back of the church disputes this, but the font may have been moved since the tablet was put up.

Inscription: 'In the earth below this tablet are the remains of James Thomson, author of the beautiful poems entitled The Seasons, Castle of Indolence, etc, who died at Richmond ... the Earl of Buchan, unwilling that so good a man and sweet a Poet should be without a memorial, has denoted the place of his interment for the satisfaction of his Admirers.

Father of Light and Life,
Thou good Supreme!
O teach me what is good,
teach me Thyself!
Save me from folly,
vanity and vice,
From every low pursuit,
and feed my soul
With knowledge,
conscious peace,
and virtue pure,
Sacred, substantial,
never fading bliss.'
(from *Winter*)

Down Under, Thomson
Is deemed a Pom's son.
Your Ozzie scoffs, 'The Pommy bummer
Thought June was summer!'

HENRY VAUGHAN

Died 1695, age 73. Buried in St Bride's churchyard, Llansantffraed, Powys. The spot is described by Siegfried Sassoon in his sonnet, At the Grave of Henry Vaughan: 'Above the voiceful windings of a river (the Usk) An old green stone of simply graven stone Shuns notice, overshadowed by a yew.'

Inscription: 'Henricus Vaughan Siluris' (followed by dates and a shield with arms of three rising suns) 'quod in sepulchrum voluit servus inutilis: peccator maximus hic iaceo✝gloria miserere'

Henry Vaughan
Prayed to be reborn.
He was not one of those who quails
At the prospect of Eternity in Wales.

OSCAR WILDE

Died 1900, age 46, after surgery on an ear infected in Reading Gaol, which led to meningitis. Being poor, he was first given a 'sixth class' burial at Bagneux, outside Paris, but posthumous royalties permitted his transfer after nine years to Père Lachaise Cemetery within the city, monument by Epstein. Though delirious, quipped, 'I am dying beyond my means'

Inscriptions: (at both Bagneux and Père Lachaise, from the Book of Job): 'Verbis meis addere nihil audebant et super illos stillabat eloquium meum' *(at Père-Lachaise) also from The Ballad of Reading Gaol:* 'And alien tears will fill for him Pity's long broken urn, For his mourners will be outcast men And outcasts always mourn.' *The monument has a door and a smother of lipstick kisses.*

**Did Oscar Wilde
Deserve to be reviled
For overlooking what a child is taught:
The importance of not being caught?**

WILLIAM WORDSWORTH

Died 1850, age 80. Caught cold and died peacefully. Buried St
Oswald's churchyard, Grasmere, Cumbria.

*Inscriptions: (at Grasmere) ND (on memorial in Westminster
Abbey) 'Blessings be with them and eternal praise Who gave us
nobler loves and nobler cares, The poets who on earth have
made us heirs Of truth and pure delight by heavenly lays!'*

**According to the young Wordsworth,
'A man travelling Third's worth
As much as one who travels First.'
An idea he later reversed.**

SIR THOMAS WYATT

Died 1542 - age probably 39, bald and black-bearded - of fever, brought on by a heat wave and journey fatigue, either whilst escorting an envoy of the Emperor Charles V from Falmouth to London, or whilst himself on an embassy to Spain. Buried in Sherborne Abbey, Dorset, in a vault under the north transept; a rather recent small tablet (15" x 12") marks the approximate spot.

Inscription, ending with Henry Howard, Earl of Surrey's epitaph: '*In memory of Sir Thomas Wyat poet and statesman who died at Clifton Maybank the house of his friend Sir John Horsey ... and was buried in the vault of this chapel. Wyat resteth here, that quick could never rest.' (An effigy of Sir John Horsey is close by.)*

**A thing about which Wyatt
Was prone to keep quiet
Was how Henry was sometimes out, and he in
With Ann Boleyn.**

W(illiam) B(utler) YEATS

Died 1939, age 73, at Roquebrune, near Monaco. Buried there temporarily, but 1948 brought home to Ireland by the Irish Navy. The rumour that the wrong man was dug up is surely scurrilous. Reburied at Drumcliff Protestant Cemetery, County Sligo, Ireland. In 1930, someone living in Steyning heard Yeats in the main street, rehearsing variations of the verse inscribed on his gravestone.

Inscription: '*Cast a cold eye On life, on death. Horseman, pass by!*'

**Flew into a paddy, Yeats
If people rhymed his name with Keats.
Any talk of 'Celtic fringes'
Knocked him right off his hinges.**

EDMUND CLERIHEW BENTLEY

last but not least, without whom the clerihew
would have been called something else. The clerihew seems to have been 'a
child of its times', the first years of the Edwardian period. Bentley first pub-
lished some clerihews in 1905. At least as early as 1904, James Elroy Flecker
was circulating rather similar verses among his Oxford contemporaries, e.g.

I am confidential adviser
To the Kaiser,
Which is rather a crusher
For the Czar of Russia.

Died 1956, age 80, in London. His son, Nicholas Bentley,
described him as 'a stickler for physical fitness, but gradually he
degenerated into a hopeless hypochondriac, and later on in life he
began to hit the bottle.' It is possible he regarded himself as
having failed to reach his potential. He was fonder than anyone
else of G K Chesterton, who illustrated many of his clerihews,
and who drew the picture of him below.

E C Bentley
Was bursting with wit, evidently.
After clerihews, for an even bigger laugh,
Wrote leaders for The Daily Telegraph.

BILL OF MORTALITY FOR A HUNDRED
ENGLISH POETS

Accidental drowning	*1*
Aftereffects of accidents	*2*
Alcohol poisoning	*1*
Apoplexy	*1*
Asthma	*1*
Blood clots, 'tumid legs'	*1*
Bloodpoisoning & sunstroke	*1*
Bronchitis, 'defluxions of rheum'	*2*
Cancer	*2*
Choking on begged bread	*1*
Consumption	*6*
Debauchery	*1*
Dropsy	*2*
Execution for treason	*1*
Exposure in open boat at sea	*1*
Fever, 'putrid feaver'	*9*
Fits	*2*
Flux (violent laxative taken in defiance of doctors' orders)	*1*
Gangrene	*1*
Gout	*6*

Heart attack/failure	*4*
Influenza	*1*
In lunatic asylums, cause unspecified	*2*
Killed in action or died of wounds	*3*
Liver disease	*1*
Malaria, 'ague', swamp fever	*3*
Meningitis	*1*
Murdered	*1*
Palsy, paralysis, strokes	*4*
Parkinson's disease	*1*
Perforated duodenum	*1*
Plague	*3*
Pneumonia	*1*
Rheumatic heart disease	*1*
Severe chill	*6*
Starvation as sole cause	*1*
Suicide	*3*
Typhoid fever	*1*
Unspecific, inc. 'gradually worn away'	*17*
Untreated for pain, in prison	*1*

NOTES ON THE CLERIHEWS

Arnold: this is pure whimsy.

Auden: his face suffered from corrugation due to a medical condition, possibly ichthyosis.

Barnes: factual; he hardly ever left his native county.

Belloc: Plausibly a defender of Latin as well as the Roman faith.

Benlowes: he rarely wrote in any other measure.

Betjeman: pure whimsy.

Blake: was indeed a role model for any poet with a yearning to be an innocent streaker.

Bloomfield: 'Beneath dread Winter's level sheets of snow, The sweet nutritious Turnip deigns to grow.' (The Farmer's Boy, Winter.)

Blunden: he did teach English literature in Japan.

Bridges: a flight of fancy, of course.

Brontë: who knows?

Brooke: the tortuous allusions are to 'some corner of a foreign field that is for ever England', and to taking tea in The Old Vicarage, Grantchester.

E B Browning: her father insisted she was an invalid and restricted her to a sedentary life at the family home in Wimpole Street, London.

R Browning: the final line is a quote from his Andrea del Sarto: 'Ah, but a man's reach should exceed his grasp, Or what's a heaven for?'

Burns: the only truth here is that the poet was not always 'off with the old love before he was on with the new.'

Byron: apocryphal. 'Knickers' are an anachronism.

Campbell: the last line quotes his poem, Pleasures of Hope. His courage as a gambler is not a matter of record, as far as I know.

Campion: the two songs referred to were written by Campion. Both are sung occasionally on BBC Radio 3.

Chatterton: fact; it was his party trick.

Chaucer: whimsy.

Chesterton: refers to his Lepanto, a narrative poem about Don John of Austria.

Clare: pretty much true, though the spoken words are not recorded.

Coleridge: the reference, of course, is to The Ancient Mariner, who as an act of penance wears the albatross he has shot around his neck.

Cowper: wrote many hymns, especially at Olney, though he lived almost two hundred years before the advent of BUPA.

Crabbe: his marriage was delayed by up to ten years by his poverty.

Day-Lewis: whimsy.

De la Mare: did use the British Museum reading room a lot; the reference is to his poem, The Listeners, which begins: Is there anybody there? said the traveller, Knocking at the moonlit door?

Donne: alludes to his love poem, The Flea, and his later recantation of love poetry to concentrate on sermons. The actual Bible verse has no relevance.

Drayton: is credited with introducing the ode form to English literature.

Dryden: it is of course a calumny to suggest that any literary scholar could ever be so inaccurate.

Duck: neither the post of Poet Laureate nor Messrs Faber and Faber existed at the time Duck lived. Was this fortunate? Dryden was the first to be appointed Poet Laureate.

Eliot: the reference is, of course, to two of his works: Old Possum's Book of Practical Cats and The Waste Land.

FitzGerald: was a bachelor and far from debauched.

Flecker: the poet knew a vast amount more about Greece than he did about the management of money.

Gay: Bertolt Brecht (1898-1956) based his Dreigroschenoper (Threepenny Opera) on Gay's The Beggars' Opera.

Goldsmith: this was his reputation.

Gray: wrote an Ode on the Death of a Favourite Cat, which drowned in a goldfish bowl. The RSPCA was not founded until 1824.

Gurney: Always poor, he would starve himself and then binge on cream buns. 'Ernie' i.e. the National Savings Bond computer, belongs to a later generation.

Hardy: Though the Mahdi staged his uprising in the Sudan during Hardy's lifetime, the mind boggles at the thought of the two discussing Hardy's nativity poem, The Oxen.

Henley: 'I am the master of my fate, I am the captain of my soul.' (Invictus)

Herbert: married in an unremarkable way.

Herrick: 'bloody' was very close to his verdict on Devon.

Hood: refers to his poem, Bridge of Sighs, which pleads with the reader to take a charitable view of a fallen woman who has thrown herself into the Thames.

Hopkins: the innovator of 'sprung rhythm'.

Housman: whether he suffered from anal discomfort is uncertain, but the remainder is fact.

Hughes: poems like View of a Pig are renowned for their uncompromising vocabulary.

Jonson: the reference is to the song Drink to me only.

Keats: literary scholars dispute whether the poet intended this revision of his famous dictum for a second edition of Hyperion.

Kipling: an invention, supposing that the poet might have referred to 'the little room' by the name of the bungalow in The Jungle Book.

Larkin: did receive five honorary D. Litt. degrees.

Lawrence: the reference is to his well-known poem, Snake.

Marvell: refers to his To his Coy Mistress, with what degree of anachronism is unknown to the author.

Masefield: whatever his poem Sea Fever may suggest to the contrary, his life as a merchant seaman was short and he was not so loath to give it up.

Meredith: was partial to words of this kind, and one can imagine a wife's reactions.

Milton: public enquiries of this kind were unknown in Milton's time; the allusion is to his Paradise Regained.

Moore: no *moore* need be said!.

Owen: true.

Plath: true enough, though arguably she had more than one bee.

Pope: only his authorship of The Dunciad is factual.

Rossetti: libellous nonsense.

Sassoon: an oblique reference to his Memoirs of a Fox-Hunting Man.

Shakespeare: whimsy.

Shelley: whimsy.

Sidney: based on legend.

Skelton: was prone to write verses like 'Warbling in the vale, Dug, dug, Jug, Jug, Good year and good luck, With chuck, chuck, chuck, chuck!'

Southey: whimsy.

Spenser: refers to the hagiographical nature of The Faerie Queene and Elizabeth I's policy of making her poets serve the body politic, or be hanged.

Stevenson: the reference is to A Child's Garden of *Verses*.

Surrey: a flight of fancy.

Swinburne: self-explanatory.

Tennyson: the queen's attitude to the poem is unknown to me.

D Thomas: the whimsy of a Gallophile.

E Thomas: whimsy, with a reference to possibly his best-known poem, Adlestrop. How lucky he was to have lived generations before the advent of the mobile phone!

Thomson: a possible view from Down-Under of his Seasons.

Vaughan: Welsh poet famous for the line, 'I saw Eternity the other night,' and elsewhere, 'Happy those early days, when I Shin'd in my angel-infancy!'

Wilde: a play, of course, on the title The Importance of Being Earnest, and an illusion to 'the love that dare not speak its name'.

Wordsworth: not factual, but not untypical of the poet's shift of mind away from republican democracy, and his opposition to invasion of his beloved Lake District by the railways.

Wyatt: based on fact. Wyatt preceded the king as Ann Boleyn's lover.

Yeats: whimsy. The fact is, there is a theory Keats may have pronounced his name so that it rhymed with Yates. The final two lines play on the concept of 'the Celtic fringe' i.e. the outlying parts of the British Isles whose cultural traditions Yeats and others were keen to revive.

Bentley: factual.

Translations of Foreign Words

Belloc: hic, hoc are different case forms of the Latin word for 'this', and sic is Latin for 'thus'. In context, we might read this as 'couldn't tell here from there, or this from that'.

Blunden   haijin is the Japanese term for a haiku poet.

E B Browning   The Italian means: 'Here wrote and died E.B.B. who, in the heart of a woman, combined scholarship with poetic spirit to forge a link between Italy and England with her golden verse. Placed here by a grateful Florence in her memory.'

Chaucer   The Latin reads: 'Geoffrey Chaucer, poet, well-known for the sacred native art of poetry, is here interred ... once the thrice-greatest poet of the English nation, GC is laid in this grave at the time appointed by God or by death; look for the signs [of his greatness] in what is spread before you. Death gives him peace as recorded on this artistic bronze.'

Chesterton   The Latin reads: 'How excellent to return to our native soil to die.'

Donne   The Latin reads: 'John Donne, theologian, teacher, poet, man of diverse and most sensitive passions from his early years, following vocation and impulse was ordained, and not unhappily so, in accordance with the holy spirit, and with the encouragement and blessing of King James in the year of Our Lord 1614 at the age of 42, assuming the role of Dean [of St Paul's] 27th November 1621; he departed this life on the last day of March 1631. Here, where his ashes settle to rest, reverence him whose name is still in the ascendant.'

Goldsmith

The Latin, by Dr Johnson, reads: 'Poets, doctors, historians, almost nobody of the writing fraternity comes anywhere near him, while those who did manage to touch him praised him beyond measure, whether moved to laughter or to tears. Powerful in his sensitivity, gentle in his guidance, exalted in disposition, animated, a great orator, shining, charming, his memory lives on in this monument. His respect for the reader [gives rise to] the love of colleagues, the faithfulness of friends.'

Housman

Hic jacet = Here lies

Pope

The Latin reads: 'who lets nothing grind him down perversely.'

Skelton

The Latin reads: 'Here lies the poet, sacred to the Muses.'

Vaughan

The Latin reads: 'Henry Vaughan the Silurian ... a useless servant who hastened to his grave; take pity on me as I lie here in the glory of God ✝ an utter sinner.'

Wilde   The inscription is from the Book of Job in the Latin Bible, Ch. 29, v. 22. We give the version from the New English Bible of 1970: 'When I had spoken, no one spoke again; my words fell gently on them.' This continues, in v. 23: 'they waited for them as for rain and drank them in like showers in spring.'

Picture credits:

Photos of the graves and/or monuments of Robert Browning, Campbell, Chaucer, Drayton, Dryden, Gay, Kipling, Masefield, Spenser and Tennyson are Copyright: Dean and Chapter of Westminster; that of Donne, Copyright: St Paul's Cathedral; those of Wilfred Owen and Edward Thomas were kindly supplied by the Commonwealth War Graves Commission; photo of Caversham Bridge (Duck), courtesy of Berks CRO; photo of Ted Hughes courtesy of the Evening Courier, Halifax; that of D H Lawrence is by Mark Lindamood; that of Vaughan by Philip Hoskins; that of Meredith by Carole Brough; that of W H Auden, by the civil authority at Kirchstetten, Austria; that of Brooke's grave by the tourist board, Skyros, Greece, and of his monument (used on the cover) by Zoe Savina; that of Burns by Dumfries Museum; that of Cowper by Glyn Jones for St Nicholas Church, East Dereham; those of Hopkins and Yeats by Treasa Macmanus; those of Byron and Hood by Madeleine Holroyd; that of Swinburne by Heather Kirk; Stevenson's is from a drawing by Norman Hale, published as a postcard for which no copyright has been traced, and appearing as the frontispiece to Laura Stubbs's Stevenson's Shrine, 1903; and the caricature of Bentley is by G K Chesterton. All remaining photos are by the Author.

Every effort has been made to trace the copyright holders, but if any have been inadvertently overlooked the publishers will be pleased to hear from them.